EVERYTHING YOU NEED TO KNOW ABOUT LENSES AND LIGHT

PHYSICS BOOK 4TH GRADE CHILDREN'S PHYSICS BOOKS

Baby Professor
EDUCATION KIDS

Speedy Publishing LLC

40 E. Main St. #1156

Newark, DE 19711

www.speedypublishing.com

Copyright 2017

In this book, we're going to talk about lenses and light. So, let's get right to it!

SCIENTIST LOOKING THROUGH A MICROSCOPE IN LABORATORY

What do all these situations have in common?

- A biologist looks through a microscope to study bacteria.

- An astronomer looks through a telescope to study the night sky.

- An audience watches a movie that's being shown using a movie projector.

- Your uncle has his eyeglass prescription changed.

- A lighthouse sends out a beam of light to warn sailors of a rocky shore.

- You pop out a contact accidentally while you're playing sports and you can't find it.

- Your friend puts a CD into his CD player and plays it for you.

- A stamp collector uses a magnifying glass to look at the details of a stamp she's thinking of buying.

- A field naturalist uses binoculars to see a rare bird up close.

- A photographer snaps a photo of a beach landscape using a vintage 35 mm camera.

ZOOM LENS

70-300 mm

1:2.8

IS USM

LENS MADE IN JAPAN

φ 77 mm

CAMERA LENS

WHAT ARE LENSES?

A single lens is made of a clear piece of glass or transparent plastic. A lens has one surface that is curved. The word "lens" comes from the word for lentil in Latin.

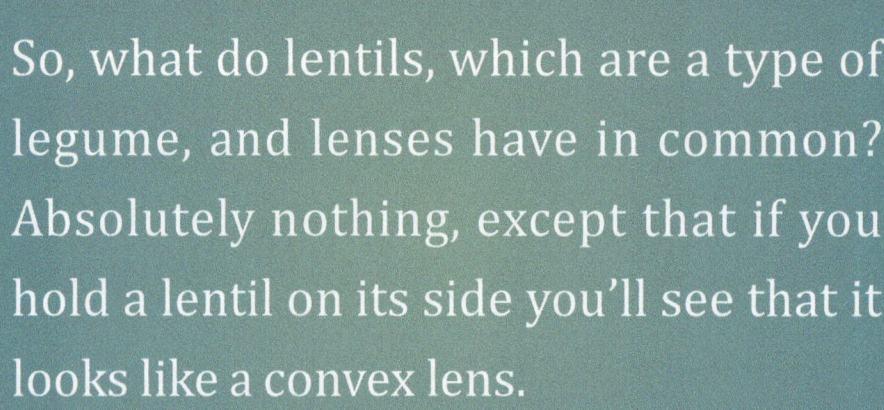

So, what do lentils, which are a type of legume, and lenses have in common? Absolutely nothing, except that if you hold a lentil on its side you'll see that it looks like a convex lens.

QUARTZ

WHO INVENTED THE LENS?

The earliest lenses were made around 750 BC with natural polished crystals, such as quartz.

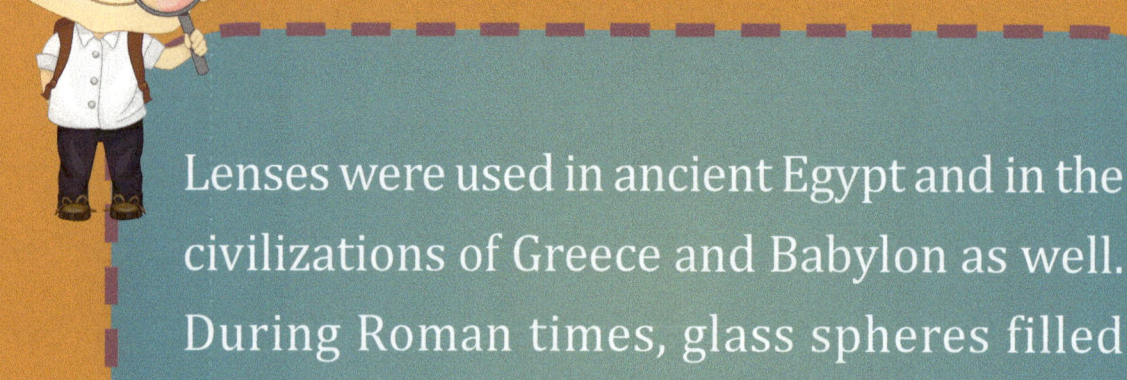

Lenses were used in ancient Egypt and in the civilizations of Greece and Babylon as well. During Roman times, glass spheres filled with water were used to make lenses.

From the 11th to the 13th century, monks used "reading stones" to help magnify the pages where they were doing artwork in books. These reading stones were very rough lenses with one flat side and one convex side.

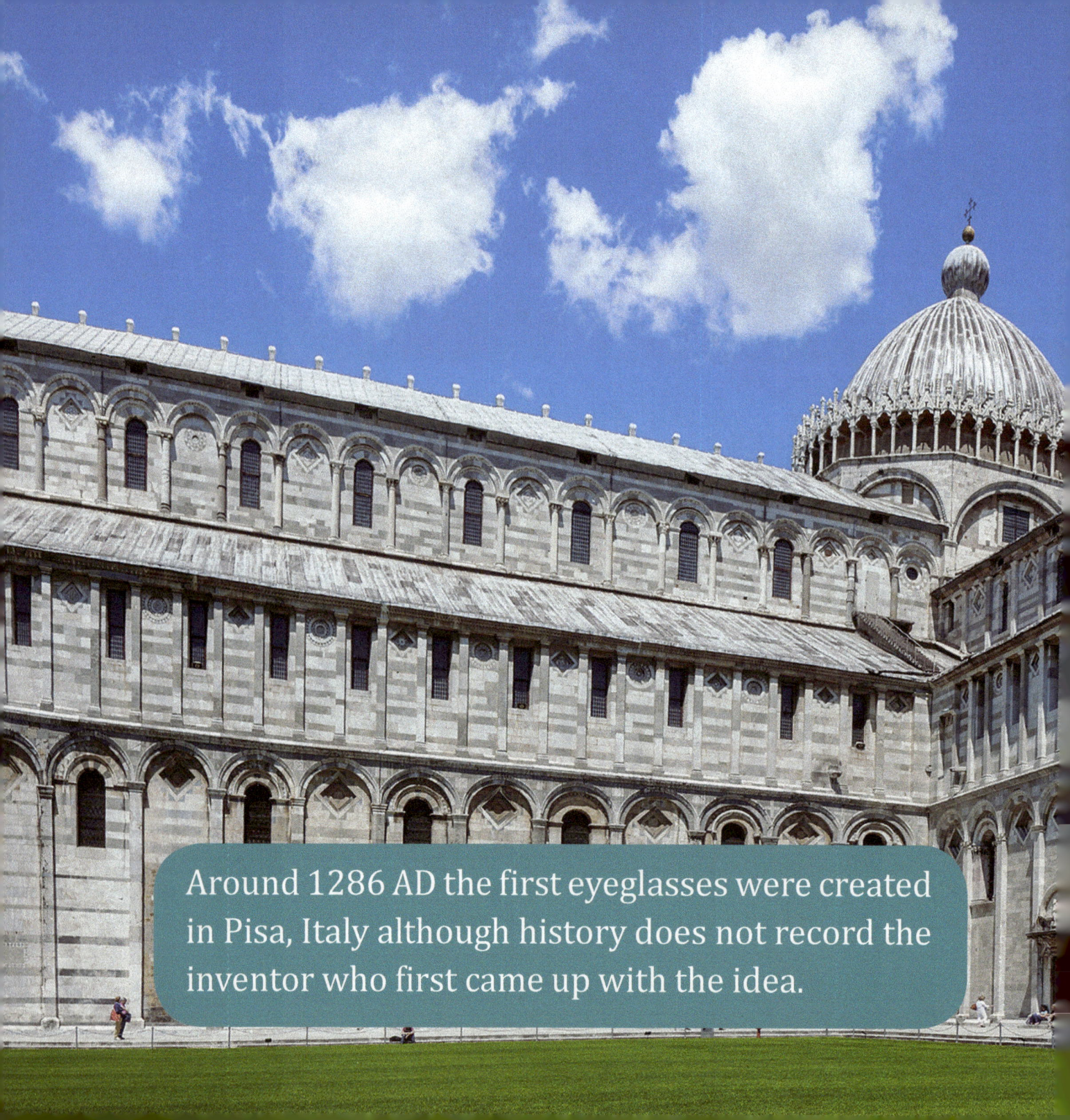

Around 1286 AD the first eyeglasses were created in Pisa, Italy although history does not record the inventor who first came up with the idea.

HOW DOES LIGHT TRAVEL?

Light behaves both as a particle and as a wave. When light rays travel from the sun, they travel through the emptiness of space in a straight line. In fact, in any situation where light travels through a vacuum, it will travel in a straight line.

A vacuum is a space that doesn't have any significant amount of matter. When light rays travel through other types of materials or from one type of substance to another, they slow down and bend.

ISN'T THE SPEED OF LIGHT A CONSTANT?

When it is traveling through a vacuum, the speed of light is a constant. It travels at 186,282 miles per second or 299,792 kilometers per second. In an hour, light would travel 670,616,629 miles. However, the speed of light does slow down if it's traveling through a substance.

If you think that this is strange, think about what happens when you run through air versus water. When you run on the beach, you can run pretty fast because you're running through air. As you run from the beach into the water, you can't keep up that same speed. The water is denser than the air so it slows you down.

Something similar happens to light. When it shines through natural water or natural crystals it slows down. It also slows down when it shines through manmade materials, such as glass or plastic.

REFRACTION

When light slows down it does something interesting. It bends and it bends differently depending on what material it's traveling through and how that material is shaped. When light bends or changes directions, it's exhibiting behavior like a wave. The bending of light is called refraction.

WHAT IS REFRACTION?

You can do a simple experiment to see refraction in action. Take a clear tall drinking glass and fill it halfway with water. Now, place a straw in the middle of the water and look at the way the straw looks at the edge where the air meets the water. You will notice that the straw in the water looks larger and isn't in a straight line with the edges of the straw above the water.

BARCODE SCANNER

The straw hasn't changed. If you take it out of the glass, you'll see that. What has changed is the way the light waves are traveling. They have slowed down and bent when they entered the water.

You can see this effect even more dramatically if you take a laser pointer and beam it at a block of plastic. As the laser beam enters the plastic it bends and it will bend again when exiting the plastic and going out into the atmosphere again.

WHAT IS THE INDEX OF REFRACTION?

Scientists use a special measurement to talk about the amount of refraction of light in specific substances. It's called the index of refraction and it's represented by the equation:

$$n = \frac{c}{v}$$

In this equation, n represents the index of refraction, c stands for the speed of light in a vacuum, which is a constant, and v represents the speed of the light in a specific substance. For example, the refraction index for water is 1.33.

This simply means that the speed of light traveling within a vacuum is about 1.33 times that of the speed it travels when it's shining through water. The index of refraction for a diamond is 2.42, which means that light travels through a vacuum at a speed about 2.42 times the speed that it travels through a diamond.

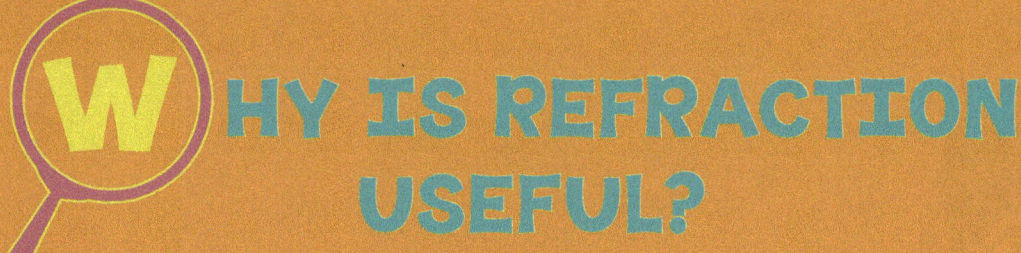

WHY IS REFRACTION USEFUL?

The way light refracts is very useful. If you wear glasses or contacts, refraction plays a part in your everyday life. The curved glass or plastic in your lenses bends the light to make it appear closer or further away depending on what type of vision correction you need.

Your eyeglasses or contacts slow down the light that comes into your eyes and makes it shift to correct for the problems with your vision. All optical equipment, such as telescopes, binoculars, and microscopes, use lenses to focus light in different ways.

TYPES OF LENSES
There are two different categories of lenses but there are many different ways the lenses can be put together.

CONVEX LENSES

The most common type is a convex lens. This is the type of lens that looks like a lentil held on its side. The curved surfaces bulge out from the center. When light rays pass through they are bent and join together to create an image at a focal point. This means the light rays converge at one point. The distance from the very center of the clear lens to the position of the focal point is called the lens's focal length.

Convex lenses can be found in both binoculars as well as telescopes.

They can bring light rays from distant points together to a concentrated focus so that you see objects far away as if they were closer.

CONCAVE LENSES

A concave lens is exactly the opposite of a convex lens. Its surfaces are "caved in" or curved inward instead of outward. Instead of bringing light rays to a focal point, it does the opposite. It spreads them out. Concave lenses are used in TV projectors to spread out light rays onto a surface.

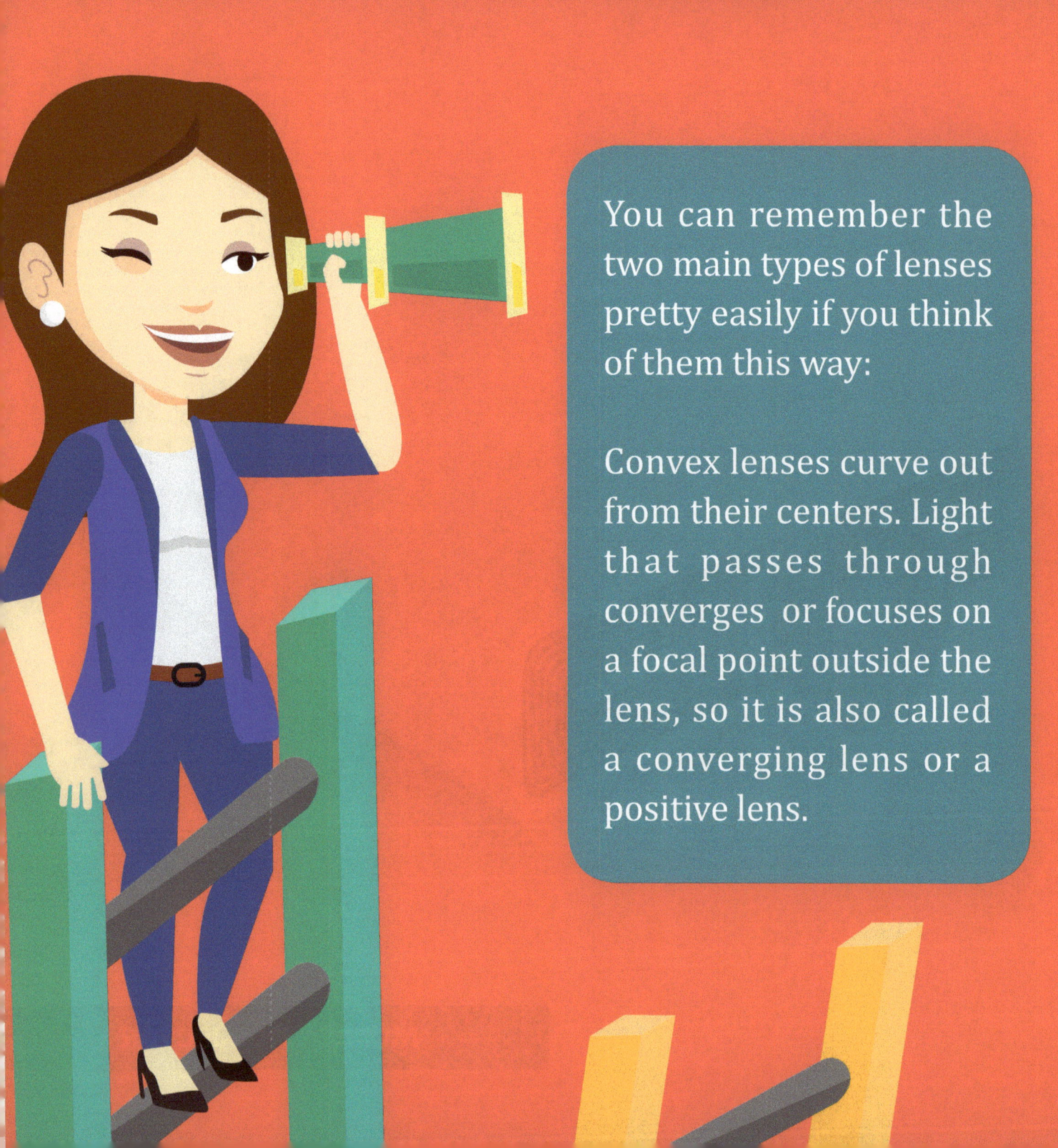

You can remember the two main types of lenses pretty easily if you think of them this way:

Convex lenses curve out from their centers. Light that passes through converges or focuses on a focal point outside the lens, so it is also called a converging lens or a positive lens.

Concave lenses curve in or cave in at their centers. Light that passes through diverges or spreads out, so it is also called a diverging lens or a negative lens.

COMPOUND LENSES

It's also possible to combine different types of lenses together for different effects. These types of lenses, made up of different types, are called compound lenses. For example, a meniscus lens has one concave side and one convex side.

CREATE A WATER LENS

Here's a fun way to create a lens from water. Work in your kitchen or bathroom so you can avoid making too much of a mess. Take a page from a magazine that no one wants. Put a thin piece of clear plastic or film on top of it so that the water you'll be using next, won't damage the page. Now experiment with dropping water droplets of different sizes using an eye-dropper or the tip of your finger. The water that you dropped on the clear plastic or film has a curved surface and will magnify the words under it.

Awesome! Now you know more about lenses and light. You can find more Physics books from Baby Professor by searching the website of your favorite book retailer.

Visit

BABY PROFESSOR
EDUCATION KIDS

www.BabyProfessorBooks.com

to download Free Baby Professor eBooks and view
our catalog of new and exciting Children's Books